The Distribution Of Energy Emitted By A Righi Vibrator

Claude Russell Fountain

In the interest of creating a more extensive selection of rare historical book reprints, we have chosen to reproduce this title even though it may possibly have occasional imperfections such as missing and blurred pages, missing text, poor pictures, markings, dark backgrounds and other reproduction issues beyond our control. Because this work is culturally important, we have made it available as a part of our commitment to protecting, preserving and promoting the world's literature. Thank you for your understanding.

Phœnix Physical Laboratory Contributions.

THE DISTRIBUTION OF ENERGY EMITTED BY A RIGHI VIBRATOR

BY

C. R. FOUNTAIN

ASSISTED BY

F. C. BLAKE

Submitted in Partial Fulfillment of the Requirements for the Degree of Doctor of Philosophy in the Faculty of Pure Science, Columbia University

Gift of
Columbia Univ.

THE DISTRIBUTION OF ENERGY EMITTED BY A RIGHI VIBRATOR.

By C. R. Fountain and F. C. Blake.

Introduction.

HERTZ[1] found that most of the energy emitted by his oscillator was radiated in the equatorial plane, that is, the plane through the spark gap and perpendicular to the axis of the oscillator; and that little or no energy was radiated in the polar direction. He mapped the direction of the electric force about the oscillator, but his results were qualitative rather than quantitative on account of the type of detector used.

In developing the theoretical side Hertz[2] failed to take into account the damping of the waves, which V. Bjerkness,[3] Hull[4] and others have shown to be large. Karl Pearson and Alice Lee[5] have shown how this factor would affect the drawings which Hertz made to represent the field about the oscillator. But they neglected the fact that there is an electrostatic field about the oscillator before the oscillation begins. A. E. H. Love[6] has considered theoretically all these factors and shown how the electric and magnetic forces may be computed for any point in the field.

It is the purpose of the present paper to show the relative amounts of energy radiated in the various directions about a Righi vibrator, and to indicate what bearing the experiments to be described have upon existing theories.

Apparatus.

The general arrangement of the apparatus is shown in Fig. 1. The vibrator V is placed at the center of the circle H. The distance

[1] Electric Waves, Eng. ed., p. 87.
[2] Electric Waves, Eng. ed., p. 141.
[3] An. der Phys., Vol. 44, pp. 81 and 513.
[4] Phys. Rev., Vol. 5, p. 231, 1897.
[5] Phil. Trans. Royal Soc. of Lon., Ser. A, V. 193, p. 158.
[6] Proc. Roy. Soc., Vol. 74, p. 73, 1904.

r of the receiver R is varied by sliding along a meter bar MM'. The angle which the radius vector at any point makes with the equatorial (vertical) plane could be varied by swinging the circle H about the axis NN' and its position at any time could be read on a graduated disk DD'. This angle will hereafter be denoted by θ.

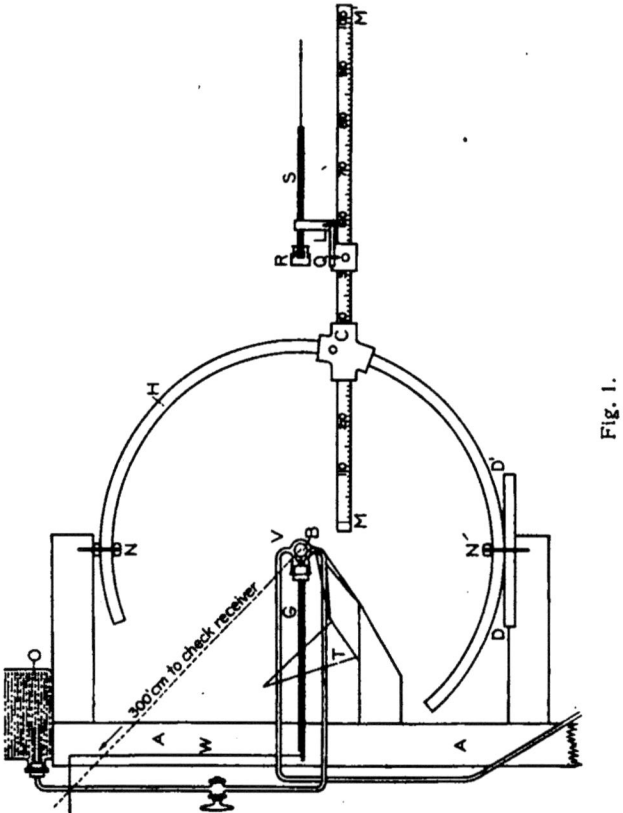

Fig. 1.

The vertical angle could be changed by sliding the clamp C about the graduated circle H. At any point the orientation of the receiver R could be changed by rotating the rod S about its axis and also by rotating the support arm L about the pivot Q. All the parts shown are drawn to scale and can be compared with the meter bar MM'. The large bottle of oil, O, on top of the support AA' supplied a constant stream of olive oil between the vibrator balls BB'

to carry off any carbon particles formed by the electrical decomposition of the oil. The brass balls BB', 2.54 cm. in diameter, were sealed with ordinary red sealing wax to the enlarged ends of the glass tubes G. These were fitted into the glass vessel V. The wires W from a 10-inch induction coil passed through the tubes G and terminated in small beads about .3 cm. from the balls B. This permitted the balls to be charged by small sparks through air. The

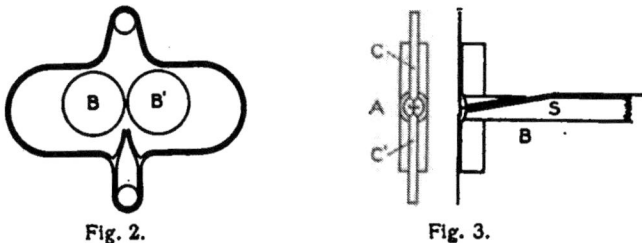

Fig. 2.   Fig. 3.

oscillation between the balls BB' took place through a small film of olive oil. An enlarged view of a vertical cross-section through the axis of the vibrator is shown in Fig. 2. This view shows the relative positions of the balls in the glass vessel. The tubes G led directly back so as to affect as little as possible the field in front of the vibrator. The triangular block T was placed to prevent interference with waves reflected from the post AA'. No metallic nails were used in constructing the apparatus.

Receiver.

The wave-detector was the type of thermo-element used in a former paper,[1] differing mainly in dimensions, but the contact between the iron and constantan wires was electrically welded instead of soldered. Fig. 3 shows two views of the receiver and R, Fig. 1, gives an end view showing the cardboard box surrounding it. The iron and constantan wires each .0025 cm. in diameter were soldered to the copper strips CC' (Fig. 3, A) crossed in the center and soldered to small copper wires which were drawn backward through the rod S (Fig. 3, B) so as to leave as little as possible (about .15 cm.) of the wires projecting at right angles to the axis of the copper strips. The total length of the receiver was 8 cm.

[1] Blake and Fountain, Phys. Rev., Vol. XXIII., No. 4, p. 257, 1906.

The strips CC' were .3 cm. wide and the length of wire between them was .35 cm.

Since a vibrator does not always give off the same amount of energy a check receiver was employed and the relative amounts of energy denoted by the ratios M/C, where M denotes the scale reading for the galvanometer connected to the main receiver and C the corresponding reading for the check receiver. To keep the two receivers from affecting each other the check receiver was placed on a shelf 3 meters distant near the focus of a spherical metallic mirror of 25 cm. diameter and 16 cm. focal length.

The same induction coil and galvanometers used in an earlier experiment[1] served in the present study.

Tests for Disturbing Factors.

Before beginning the exploration of the field it was necessary to make sure that no disturbing factors were neglected. A few of the more important tests are here given:

1. When the two spheres B, B' were made to touch each other and the induction coil put in operation, no effect could be detected in either galvanometer unless one of the receivers was within 10 cm. of a lead wire W.

2. Notwithstanding this a further test for effects from the induction coil was made by taking readings with the coil in various orientations at its regular distance of 400 cm. from the vibrator and 900 cm. from the galvanometers. The greatest variation in the ratios M/C, even when the main receiver was at the pole so as to receive but little of the energy radiated from the vibrator, was less than 5 per cent. The coil was then placed permanently in the position to give least effect.

3. The vibrator axis was set obliquely to the walls of the room so as to avoid all chance of stationary waves and disturbing reflections. Later tests showed the complete absence of any energy reflected from surrounding objects except a small amount reflected from the post AA', Fig. 1. The triangular block T was inserted to divert these reflections.

4. The ratio M/C should be constant for all points equidistant in

[1] Blake and Fountain, l. c.

the equatorial plane. This was true for all angles from 45° below the horizontal to 85° above, except in the neighborhood of 45° above when an increase of nearly 4 per cent. was observed for a distance of 20 cm. For this region however it was impossible to cut off the reflections from the post AA' without interfering with the waves en route to the check receiver.

5. One of the most troublesome disturbances and one not discovered for some time was the effect of one receiver upon the other. Further experiments showed that a copper strip, the same length as a receiver, when placed in the vicinity of the vibrator might increase or decrease the ratio M/C by 50 per cent. In other words the receivers reradiate most of the energy they receive. It was for this reason that the check receiver was placed so far away near the focus of a spherical mirror. It was slightly displaced from the focus so that the energy reradiated from it would be brought to a focus somewhere above the horizontal plane. If the main receiver were 5 cm. from the vibrator the energy reradiated from it would be brought to focus sufficiently near the check receiver to nearly double its readings. If placed 10 cm. away, however, the effect could scarcely be detected. But to make sure that no effect of this kind should enter the final readings no attempt has been made to explore the field within a distance of 14.4 cm.

6. The galvanometer wires leading to the thermal junction were closely twisted to within about .7 cm. from the thermal junction. But if these twisted wires formed a loop where the field was strong and projected in the direction of the electric force it might absorb nearly as much energy as the receiver itself. That is, if the receiver axis were perpendicular to the electric force and a loop of about 3 cm. diameter were parallel to the electric force, the galvanometer deflection might be nearly as large as when the receiver was in the position to absorb the most energy. These lead wires had therefore to be carefully straightened.

7. Another effect mentioned in a former paper[1] as the aging of the vibrator had to be taken into account. The ratio M/C does not remain constant for successive readings when the positions of the receivers remain the same. After the vibrator had been cleaned

[1] Blake and Fountain, l. c.

TABLE I.

Swinging Curve at 15 cm. August 7, 1906, 2 P. M.
Resistance of main = 1.749 ohms. Shunts, 6 and 10.
Resistance of check = 1.889 ohms. Receiver faced.
Standard value for 0-0-15 is 27.80.

Main.			Check.			Ratios.			
Zero.	Turning Point.	Def.	Zero.	Turning Point.	Def.	M/C	Mean.	Standard Mean.	Correct'd Mean.
	0-0-15								
406	44	362	159	72	87	4.17	4.20	6.62	27.80
404	54	350	157	74	83	4.22			
	0-15-15								
408	75	333	158	74	84	3.97−	3.97		26.18
407	157	250	158	95	63	3.97			
	0-345-15								
402	20	382	156	63	93	4.11	4.12		27.02
403	40	363	157	69	88	4.13			
	0-0-15								
402	58	344	155	74	81	4.25	4.25	6.54	27.80
403	12	391	155	63	92	4.25			
	0-60-15								
401	281	120	153	73	80	1.50	1.50		9.70
404	304	100	155	88	67	1.49			
	0-300-15								
401	288	113	152	72	80	1.41+	1.42		9.08
402	281	121	152	67	85	1.42+			
	0-0-15								
402	73	329	149	74	75	4.38	4.39	6.33	27.80
399	82	317	150	78	72	4.40			
	0-30-15								
403	113	290	153	71	82	3.54	3.55		22.40
404	98	306	155	69	86	3.56			
	0-45-15								
402	192	210	154	75	79	2.66	2.66		16.75
401	202	199	154	79	75	2.65+			
	0-0-15								
399	43	356	153	72	81	4.39	4.42	6.29	27.80
401	36	365	155	73	82	4.45			
	0-75-15								
401	360	41	153	84	69	.594	.598		3.74
400	358.5	41.5	153	84	69	.602			
	0-90-15								
400	391	9	154	72	82	.110	.112		.69
400	390	10	154	66	88	.114			
	0-0-15								
398	55	343	152	76	76	4.52	4.52	6.15	27.80
402	53	349	155	78	77	4.53			

and bright surfaces of the balls brought into the sparking position, the ratio M/C would either steadily increase or decrease according to circumstances. But after it had been run for sometime this variation was no longer a steady one. In the former paper we offered a possible explanation of this which seemed to fit all our earlier observations. However, later observations showed that the explanation was far from complete; for when a rigid test was made,

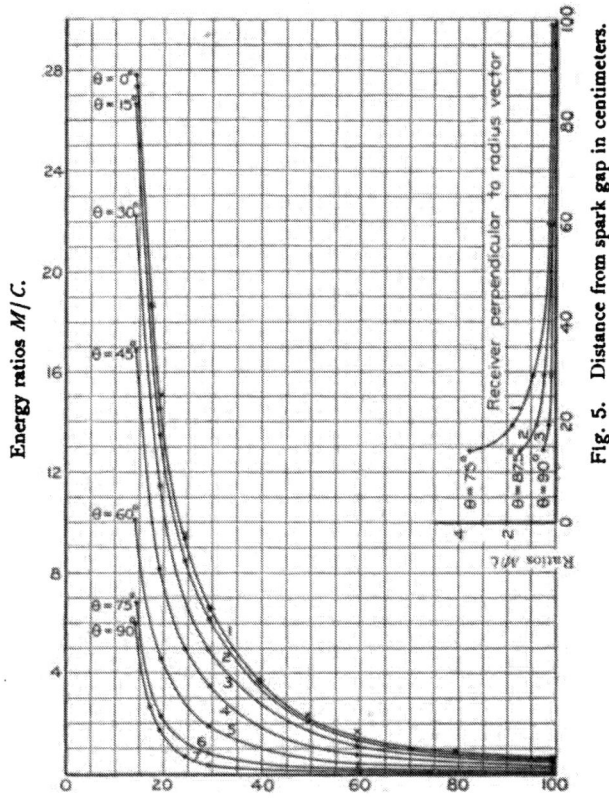

Distance from spark gap in centimeters.

Fig. 4. The angle θ opposite the first point on each curve represents the angle between the radius vector and the equatorial plane. The orientation of the receiver is such that maximum energy is received. · The crosses indicate points for curve 1 as calculated from the empirical formula in Table II.

the ratio M/C steadily decreased for conditions which seemed identical with those which had previously shown the greatest increase.

At present it seems probable that the wearing away of the balls at the spark gap causes a slight change in the wave-length emitted. Unless the two receivers are tuned to exactly the same wave-length, any change in the wave-length emitted will affect each receiver differently, thus changing the ratio M/C. But whatever the cause may be the effect had to be taken into account. Since

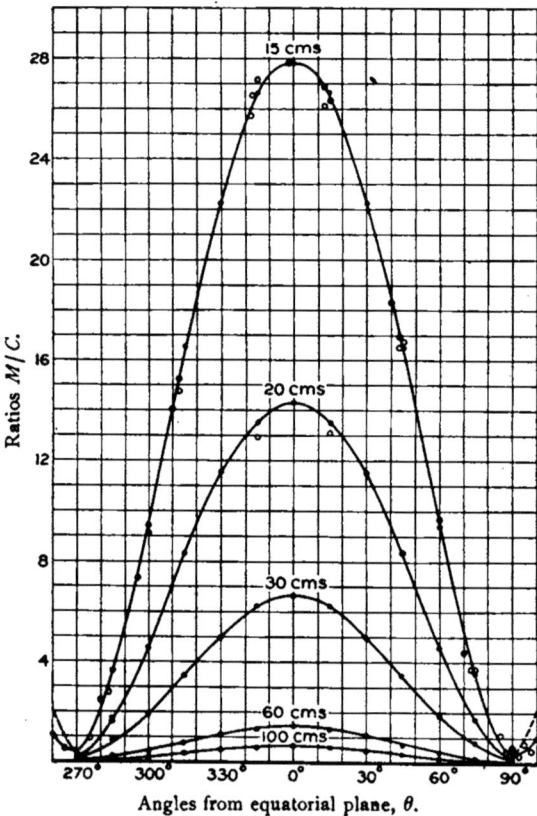

Fig. 6. In each curve the receiver is at a constant distance from the spark-gap. The receiver's axis is always perpendicular to the radius vector. Black dots show mean of all observations for a given angle from the equatorial plane. Circles show individual observations which gave greatest variation from this mean.

the variation showed itself to be a definite linear one for a short time after the vibrator was cleaned, a standard position for the main receiver was chosen and returned to after every fourth setting. The ratios for the intermediate positions were allowed their percentage increase or decrease as shown by the two values for the standard position. To get a complete curve before the deterioration became variable only two or three readings were taken for each setting.

The effective resistance of the thermal junctions varied with the temperature of the room, therefore the ratios M/C for any one posi-

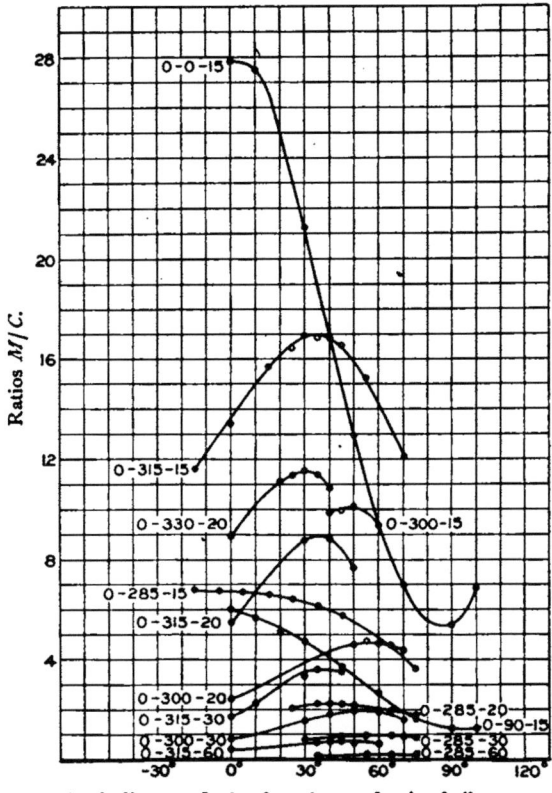

Fig. 7. The orientation of the receiver is changed while its position in the field remains constant.

tion varied from day to day. This ratio also depended upon the galvanometer shunts used. A standard value (27.80) was chosen for the position (0°–0°–15 cm.) of the main receiver. The first figure in denoting the position of the receiver refers to the angle from the horizontal plane measured on the vertical circle H. The second figure denotes the angle from the equatorial plane, that is the angle θ. The last figure shows the distance (r) in cms. of the middle of the receiver from the spark gap.

The preceeding sample set of observations shows how the various corrections were made to the observed ratios.

Experimental Results.

Curve 1, Fig. 4, is the standard curve upon which all other curves are based. The receiver was kept in the horizontal and equatorial planes while the distance alone was varied. The ratios here determined for the various distances are used as the standard values for all the swinging curves in Fig. 6.

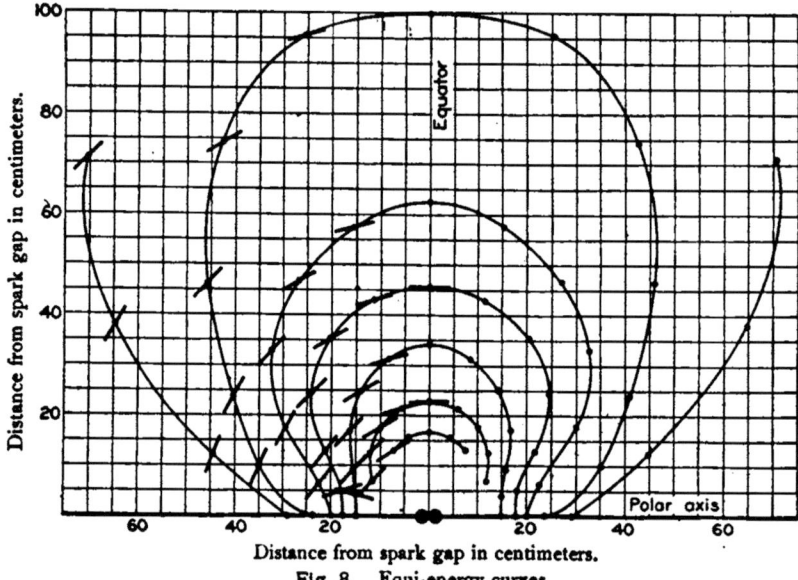

Fig. 8. Equi-energy curves.

The direction curves, Fig. 7, show the direction of the resultant electric force at the various points and the maximum values for such positions. Curves 2 to 6, Fig. 4, were obtained by a combination of the curves in Fig. 7 with those in Fig. 6. The curves in Fig. 5 were obtained directly from those in Fig. 6. The points on the equi-energy curves in Fig. 8 were found by taking arbitrary values for the ratios and ascertaining from the curves in Fig. 4 at what distance those ratios would be found for various angles. That is, Fig. 8 shows the electric field in the horizontal plane through the vibrator plotted with lines drawn through points which receive the same amount of energy. Each curve runs through the positions at which the energy intensity is twice that for points lying on the curve next beyond it. In one half of the field the orienta-

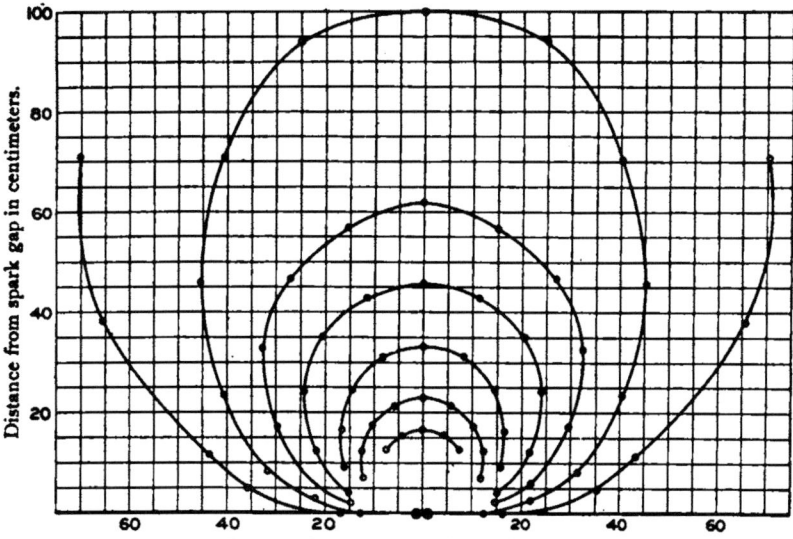

Fig. 9. Equi-energy curves. Receiver everywhere perpendicular to radius vector.

tion of the receiver for maximum energy is shown. In general this direction is at right angles to the radius vector at that point. In the polar direction ($\theta = 90°$), however, this is not true, nor is it

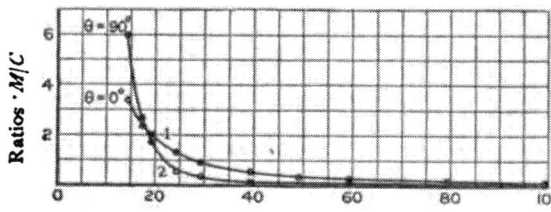

Fig. 10. Radial distance curves.

true for some of the other angles when the receiver is near the vibrator. For example, when $\theta = 75°$ the axis of the receiver must be directed toward the vibrator when $r = 15$ cm., but conforms to the general rule when $r > 50$ cm.

TABLE II.

Assume $E = K^2 \dfrac{\cos^2\theta}{r^2} + k^2 \dfrac{\sin^2\theta}{r^4}$, *where* $K = 75.25$, $k = 495$.

Distance. r	$\theta = 0°$ Obs.	$\theta = 0°$ Cal.	$\theta = 15°$ Obs.	$\theta = 15°$ Cal.	$\theta = 30°$ Obs.	$\theta = 30°$ Cal.	$\theta = 45°$ Obs.	$\theta = 45°$ Cal.	$\theta = 60°$ Obs.	$\theta = 60°$ Cal.	$\theta = 75°$ Obs.	$\theta = 75°$ Cal.	$\theta = 90°$ Obs.	$\theta = 90°$ Cal.
14.4	27.80	27.30	26.65	25.91	22.25	21.84	16.90	16.47	10.11	11.10	6.80	7.11	5.98	5.65
17.4	18.70	18.70		17.36		14.68		10.67		6.65		3.72	2.63	2.64
19.4	14.50	15.04	13.48	14.19	11.45	11.71	8.17	8.38	4.58	5.04	2.22	2.60	1.73	1.71
24.4	9.36	9.51	8.58	8.94		7.31	4.95	5.10		2.89		1.28	.65	.68
29.4	6.63	6.55	6.20	6.15	4.91	5.00	3.44	3.44	1.86	1.88	.85*	.75	.32	.33
39.4	3.74	3.65		3.42		2.77		1.88		.99		.34	.12	.10
49.4	2.03	2.32		2.17		1.75		1.18		.61		.19		.04
59.4	1.43	1.69	1.31	1.50	1.09	1.20	.72	.81	.40	.42	.18	.13	.05	.02
79.4	.92	.90		.84		.68		.45		.23		.07		.008
99.4	.62	.57	.59	.53	.47	.43	.34	.29	.19	.14	.10	.04	.03	.003

In Fig. 9 the equi-energy curves are drawn just as in Fig. 8, except that the receiver has its axis everywhere perpendicular to the radius vector. The curves in Fig. 5 must here be used instead of curves 6 and 7 of Fig. 4.

When $\theta = 0$ and the axis of the receiver is radial the energy absorbed is shown in curve 1, Fig. 10, while curve 2 shows the effect when the receiver is radial in the polar axis ($\theta = 90°$).

The polarization of the waves seems to vary with the distance from the vibrator. Thus at 0-0-15 only 2.7 per cent. as much energy was found when the receiver was perpendicular to the horizontal plane as when it was perpendicular to the equatorial plane. For 0-0-30 the corresponding percentage was 4.6, while at 0-0-60 it was 9.7 per cent.

An empirical formula was found to represent approximately the maximum energy for any point in the field. Table II. shows the corresponding observed and calculated values. The degree of agreement between this formula and the one developed later from purely theoretical considerations will be discussed later.

For points where there is only a very small amount of energy the deflections of the galvanometers due to magnetic and other disturbances render the observations quite inaccurate. That part of Table II. enclosed within the heavy lines includes those observations which are apt to be especially inaccurate. The position marked with a star (*) is not trustworthy because the only readings taken at that point were at a time when the deterioration factor was quite large and irregular. The energy recorded for that part of the field near the vibrator where the radial and the transverse components of the forces have about the same effect will probably be too small, for the receiver cannot be turned so as to get the full effect of either force.

THEORETICAL DISCUSSION.

Assuming that the field about a Righi vibrator is similar to the field about a theoretical electric doublet the forces in the field may be represented as has been done by A. E. H. Love.[1] That is the transverse component of the electric force is

---

[1] A. E. H. Love, Proc. Royal Soc., Vol. 74, p. 73, 1904.

$$F = \frac{\cos\theta}{r^3} A e^{-\frac{\nu}{\lambda}(ct-r)} \left[\left(1 - \frac{r\nu}{\lambda} + \frac{r^2(\nu^2 - 4\pi^2)}{\lambda^2}\right) \sin\frac{2\pi}{\lambda}(ct - r + \epsilon) \right.$$
$$\left. + \frac{2\pi r}{\lambda}\left(1 - \frac{2r\nu}{\lambda}\right) \cos\frac{2\pi}{\lambda}(ct - r + \epsilon) \right], \quad (1)$$

when $ct > r$, and when $ct < r$ it is

$$F = \frac{\cos\theta}{r^3} A \sin\frac{2\pi\epsilon}{\lambda}. \quad (2)$$

Where θ is the angle between the radius vector and the equatorial plane, r the distance along the radius vector, A a constant depending upon the amplitude of vibration, ν the damping constant, λ the wave-length, c the velocity of radiation, t the time from the beginning of the oscillation, and ϵ a constant depending upon the phase between the electric and magnetic forces.

The radial component of the electric force is

$$R = \frac{2\sin\theta}{r^3} A e^{-\frac{\nu}{\lambda}(ct-r)} \left[\left(1 - \frac{r\nu}{\lambda}\right) \sin\frac{2\pi}{\lambda}(ct - r + \epsilon) \right.$$
$$\left. + \frac{2\pi r}{\lambda} \cos\frac{2\pi}{\lambda}(ct - r + \epsilon) \right], \quad (3)$$

when $ct > r$, and

$$R = \frac{2\sin\theta}{r^3} A \sin\frac{2\pi\epsilon}{\lambda}, \quad (4)$$

when $ct < r$.

The transverse component of the magnetic force is

$$H = -\frac{\cos\theta}{r^2} A e^{-\frac{\nu}{\lambda}(ct-r)} \left[\left(\frac{\nu}{\lambda} - \frac{r(\nu^2 - 4\pi^2)}{\lambda^2}\right) \sin\frac{2\pi}{\lambda}(ct - r + \epsilon) \right.$$
$$\left. - \frac{2\pi}{\lambda}\left(1 - \frac{2r\nu}{\lambda}\right) \cos\frac{2\pi}{\lambda}(ct - r + \epsilon) \right], \quad (5)$$

when $ct > r$, but vanishes for $ct < r$.

The radial component of the magnetic force is everywhere equal to zero.

If these represent the true values for the forces, the current produced by them at any point in a conductor placed in the field can be determined. Consider the receiver in the equatorial plane with its axis parallel to the axis of the vibrator. The forces in the field are practically the same about every point in the receiver. So the average force about the receiver is proportional to the force at any particular point in it, if it be more than 14 cm. from the vibrator. The current at any point in the receiver will be proportional to the forces about any particular point in it. That is, the rate of change with the distance is practically the same for all the forces about the receiver. Therefore the current at the thermal junction will be proportional to the forces in the immediate neighborhood of the junction. The deflections of the galvanometers will be proportional to the heat developed at the thermal junction; that is, proportional to the square of the current at the junction.

$$\therefore \text{Heat} \propto \int_0^\infty i^2 dt \propto \int_{r/c}^\infty (F^2 + H^2) dt.$$

Since $\tan 2\pi\epsilon/\lambda = 2\pi/\nu$,[1]

$$\int_{r/c}^\infty (F^2+H^2)dt = \frac{\cos^2\theta}{r^2} A^2 \frac{2\pi^2}{c\nu\lambda^3}(4\pi^2+\nu^2)\left[1 - \frac{2\nu\lambda^3}{r^3(4\pi^2+\nu^2)^2} + \frac{\lambda^4(4\pi^2+5\nu^2)}{2r^4(4\pi^2+\nu^2)^3}\right]. \quad (6)$$

Within the region explored the last two terms in the brackets could never be larger than .0002. Therefore the electromagnetic energy will be approximately proportional to $\cos^2\theta/r^2$. This is identical with the empirical equation in Table II.

Let us now consider what effect the radial forces will have upon the receivers. If the main receiver is in the polar region ($\theta = 90°$) with its axis parallel to the radius vector the only force acting along its axis will be the radial component of the electric force. Again assuming that the current at the junction is proportional to the forces immediately surrounding that point, the energy absorbed will be proportional to

$$\int_{r/c}^\infty R^2 dt = \frac{A^2\pi}{2c\nu\lambda} \frac{\sin^2\theta}{r^4}\left[1 - \frac{\lambda}{r}\frac{4\nu}{(4\pi^2+\nu^2)} + \frac{\lambda^2(4\pi^2+5\nu^2)}{r^2(4\pi^2+\nu^2)^3}\right]. \quad (7)$$

Calculating the value of ν from the interference curves obtained by Willard and Woodman[1] for waves 20 cm. long it seems probable that the value of ν is not greater than .15. Substituting this value

[1] See Love, l. c.

in (7) the last two terms in the brackets become larger than .02 for $r = 15$ cm. but only .001 when $r = 30$ cm.

The values in the last column of Table II. were calculated from the equation $E = k^2/r^4$, where k was 495. If the last two terms of (7) be introduced and k be given the value 489 the figures for the last column of Table II. become respectively, 5.72, 2.65, 1.71, .68, .32, .10, .04, .02, .008, .003. These show a slightly better agreement with the observed values. The value assumed for ν is prob-

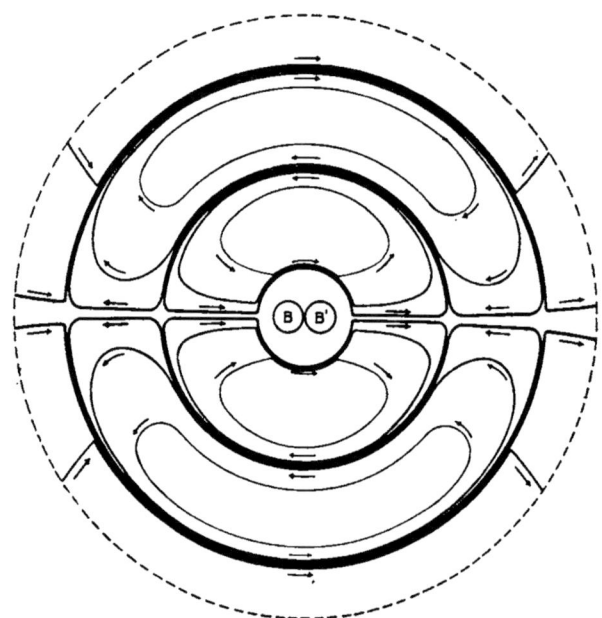

Fig. 11. Lines of electric force.

ably too large. A smaller value would give still better agreement.

The assumption that the current at the junction is proportional to the forces at that point is probably not strictly true. When $r = 15$ cm. the value of R at the center of the receiver is certainly not proportional to the average value of R for the entire length of the receiver. As the charges begin to build up at the ends of the receiver the forces of their mutual repulsion increase so as to oppose the force R with increasing effectiveness for increasing distance from the center of the receiver. To compute the effect of these repulsive forces would require a better knowledge of the number of free electrons in the copper strips and their behavior under oscillating forces than the authors have at present. Some idea of the extent to which these forces counteract the effect of the forces in the field near the ends of the receiver may be seen by neglecting these forces and computing the ratio of energy absorbed when $r = 15$ cm. to that absorbed when $r = 30$ cm. There is a 40 per cent. variation from the observed ratio. The error involved for the corresponding distances in assuming that the current at the junction is proportional to the value of R at that point is probably less than 4 per cent.

The physical significance of the radial force may be seen from Fig. 11, where the lines of force are plotted for

$$t = \frac{\frac{3}{2}\lambda - \varepsilon}{c}.$$

The three values for the intensity of the force here plotted are to each other as 10,000 : 100 : 10. The dotted circle is $\frac{3}{2}\lambda$ from the spark-gap. Lines are drawn up to a distance of $\frac{1}{4}\lambda$ although the formula used probably does not hold so near to such a vibrator. As the energy flows into the polar region from the two halves of the field the electric forces in the two approaching waves will always be in the same relative direction. But since the direction of the energy flow is opposite in the two cases the magnetic forces must be opposed to each other. Therefore if the two halves of the field were symmetrical there would be at any point on the polar axis a varying electric force, but the resultant magnetic force would always be equal to zero. Prof. G. F. FitzGerald[1] made this case the basis of an article on the "Longitudinal Component in Light."

When the receiver is in the polar region ($\theta = 90°$) with its axis perpendicular to the polar axis the energy absorbed varies approximately as $1/r^4$ and therefore might suggest that it was due to some effect of the force R upon the lead wires. Varying the positions of the lead wires produced only slight changes in the energy absorbed. The transverse components of the electric and magnetic forces become equal to zero when $\theta = 90°$. But the ends of a receiver 8

[1] Phil. Mag., Vol. 42, p. 266, 1896.

cm. long reach out on either side into the field where there is a force component toward the middle of the receiver. This is readily seen from Fig. 11. The forces at the two ends would at the same instant be both directed toward the center so that the only flow must be from the ends of the receiver past the thermal junction into the capacity of the galvanometer circuit and out again. If such a current were proportional to the forces at the ends of the receiver the heat developed at the junction would vary approximately as shown in curve 3, Fig. 5. The whole effect is so small that its exact nature is very difficult to determine.

When θ is 0° and the receiver radial the energy absorbed varies as $1/r^2$, that is in the same way as when the receiver is perpendicular to the radius vector. Varying the lead wires failed to reveal the cause for an absorption of energy as great as shown by curve 1, Fig. 10. The radial component of the electric force should be zero for this position, and the axis of the receiver is perpendicular to both the electric and magnetic forces. No satisfactory explanation for this phenomenon has yet been found.

Conclusions.

The results of the present investigation seem to indicate:

1. That in computing the total energy in the field about a Righi vibrator it is necessary to consider the radial component of the electric force as well as the transverse components of the electric and magnetic forces.

2. That the electromagnetic waves spread out from the spark gap in such a manner that the energy at any point is approximately proportional to the square of the cosine of the angle between the radius vector and the equatorial plane and inversely proportional to the square of the distance from the spark gap.

3. That the energy due to the radial component of the electric force varies approximately as the square of the sine of the angle between the radius vector and the equatorial plane and inversely as the fourth power of the distance from the spark gap.

4. That in order to receive the maximum energy the thermal element of the Klemenčič type should everywhere be perpendicular to the radius vector except near the poles, where it should be parallel to the radius vector.

5. That the thermal element used in these experiments when placed in the equatorial plane with its axis parallel to the direction of propagation of the electromagnetic waves absorbs more than 14 per cent. as much energy as when it is in the resonating position.

6. That this type of receiver absorbs a small amount of energy when it is on the polar axis and perpendicular to it, and therefore perpendicular to the radius vector.

7. That two such receivers in the same field greatly influence each other.

8. That a Righi vibrator does not continue to give out wave-trains of the same strength or character as shown by its "deterioration" with use.

9. That the waves from a Righi vibrator appear to become less plane polarized as they proceed from the vibrator.

10. That a theory based upon the assumption that the waves from a Righi vibrator are identical with those from a vibrating "electric doublet" and also that the thermal element of the Klemenčič type acts as a "point receiver" holds with a fair degree of accuracy up to within $\frac{3}{4}\lambda$ from the vibrator.

We wish to thank Mr. J. B. Blanchard and others for their assistance in taking measurements. To Professor Hallock and Professor Wills we are indebted for their suggestions and friendly interest. Our acknowledgments are especially due to Professor E. F. Nichols who suggested the problem and some of the methods for solving it.

PHŒNIX PHYSICAL LABORATORIES,
COLUMBIA UNIVERSITY,
April, 1907.

Printed by Libri Plureos GmbH in Hamburg, Germany